FAST Lane
DRAG RACING

PRO STOCK
DRAGSTERS

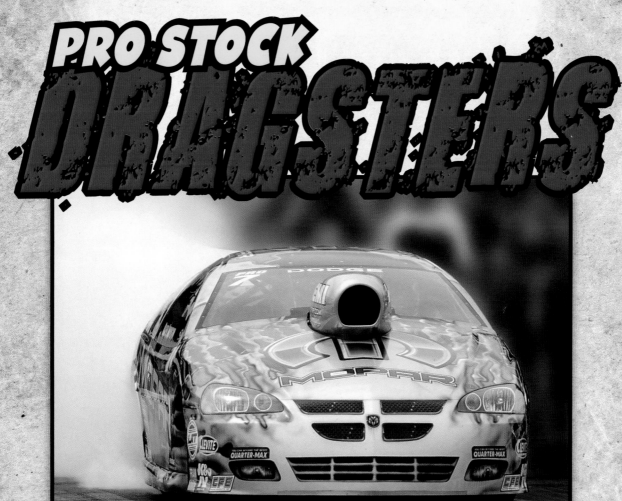

By Tyrone Georgiou

Gareth Stevens
Publishing

Please visit our Web site, www.garethstevens.com. For a free color catalog of all our high-quality books, call toll free 1-800-542-2595 or fax 1-877-542-2596.

Library of Congress Cataloging-in-Publication Data

Georgiou, Tyrone.
 Pro stock dragsters / Tyrone Georgiou.
     p. cm. — (Fast lane, drag racing)
 Includes index.
 ISBN 978-1-4339-4700-1 (pbk.)
 ISBN 978-1-4339-4701-8 (6-pack)
 ISBN 978-1-4339-4699-8 (library binding)
 1. Drag racing. 2. Dragsters. I. Title.
 GV1029.3.G49 2011
 796.72—dc22
                                            2010032327

First Edition

Published in 2011 by
Gareth Stevens Publishing
111 East 14th Street, Suite 349
New York, NY 10003

Copyright © 2011 Gareth Stevens Publishing

Designer: Daniel Hosek
Editor: Greg Roza

Photo credits: Cover, pp. 1, 9, 11, 13, 14–15, 19 Rusty Jarett/Getty Images; p. 5 Alvis Upitis/Getty Images; pp. 7, 17 (main image) Brian Bahr/Getty Images; p. 15 (inset) Jamie Squire/Getty Images; p. 17 (inset) Larry Caruso/WireImage/Getty Images.

Printed in the United States of America

CPSIA compliance information: Batch #CW11GS: For further information contact Gareth Stevens, New York, New York at 1-800-542-2595.

CONTENTS

Words in the glossary appear in **bold** type the first time they are used in the text.

LET'S DRAG RACE!

Drag racing is a contest between two motor **vehicles** racing side by side. The driver who crosses the finish line first wins.

Drag racing became an official sport in the early 1950s. Drivers took their **"hot rods"** to California's Mohave Desert to race. Soon they raced on airport runways in Southern California. Now, drivers race on short, straight tracks all over the country.

Today, there are many kinds of drag racing. One of these is called Pro Stock.

Fast Fact

In 1987, Bill Kuhlmann became the first **IHRA** racer to surpass 200 miles (322 km) per hour in a race car that had doors like a street car.

Early Pro Stock cars looked different from today's cars, but they were just as much fun to watch.

WHAT'S A PRO STOCK CAR?

Pro Stock dragsters look like cars you see on the street. However, they're very different on the inside. Sometimes called "factory hot rods," Pro Stock cars are specially built race cars.

The body of a Pro Stock car is built of steel. It has doors that open just like regular cars do. Underneath the body is a frame made of steel tubes that are **welded** together. A **roll cage** keeps the driver safe in case the car flips over.

Pro Stock racer Mike Edwards drives a Pontiac GPX.

Fast Fact Pro Stock cars are made using a template, or pattern, of the street cars they are supposed to look like. There are templates for Ford, Chevrolet, and Dodge cars.

Pro Stock cars use **V-8** engines much like those in cars of the 1950s and 1960s. They use gasoline for **fuel**. That gasoline has an **octane** rating of 118, which means it's very powerful. The regular gasoline people buy for their cars has a rating of only 87!

There's a huge scoop on the hood of the car to force large amounts of air into the engine. The air and high-octane fuel combine to make a lot of **horsepower** (HP).

scoop

Johnny Gray drives up to the starting line at zMAX Dragway in Concord, North Carolina.

Fast Fact
Headlights and taillights are standard parts on Pro Stock cars. They must be in the same places they are on regular cars.

PRO STOCK TIRES

Pro Stock car tires are called "slicks." Unlike regular tires, they're smooth and sticky. This helps the car speed down the track. The rear tires are bigger than the front tires because the engine powers them. They're 17 inches (43 cm) wide! The front tires are only used to steer the car.

The back tires create a lot of **traction** at the beginning of a race. This can cause the front end to go up. "Wheelie bars" keep the front end down and help the driver control the car.

Without wheelie bars, dragsters could flip over!

wheelie bar

Fast Fact New kinds of wheelie bars for Pro Stock cars weigh less than they did in the past. Even a small difference in weight can help a car go faster.

PRO STOCK CARS ON THE TRACK

Good traction at the beginning of a race helps a driver get a quick start. Getting a quick start gives a driver a better chance of winning. To get the best traction, a driver needs to heat his rear tires and the track. So the driver does a "burnout." Water is sprayed on the track, and the driver **revs** the engine and drives through it. This makes a lot of smoke and noise. It's one of the coolest sights in drag racing!

Racer Warren Johnson does a burnout before a race.

13

Pro Stock races take place on a ¼-mile (400-m) track. The drivers get into position on the starting line in a process called staging. This is done with the help of the starting tree. The starting tree is a pole in the center of the starting line. It has lights that stick out like the branches on a tree. Drivers are given the green light to start. A driver who starts too soon "red lights" and loses the race.

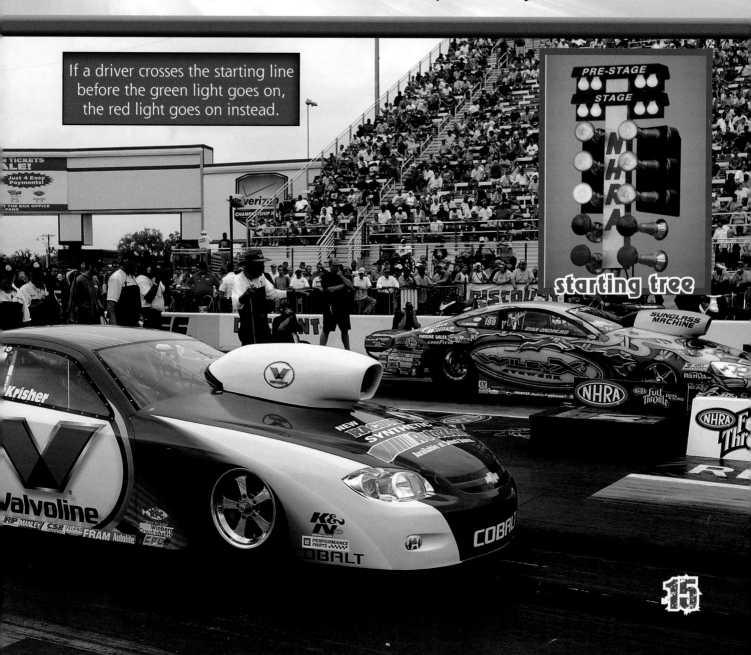

Fast Fact

Erica Enders is an up-and-coming Pro Stock driver. She started her racing career at age 8 in Jr. dragsters. Her life story was made into the Disney movie *Right on Track*.

If a driver crosses the starting line before the green light goes on, the red light goes on instead.

starting tree

GOING FOR THE WIN

A driver must do a lot very quickly during a race. A Pro Stock race takes just 7 seconds! Drivers have to shift gears and speed up at just the right time. Then they need to slow the car down from 200 miles (322 km) per hour to 0. Brakes alone can't do this, so drivers "pop the chutes"! Pro Stock cars have special **parachutes** to slow them down and make sure they don't go flying off the end of the track.

Warren Johnson

Don't blink! You might miss the entire race!

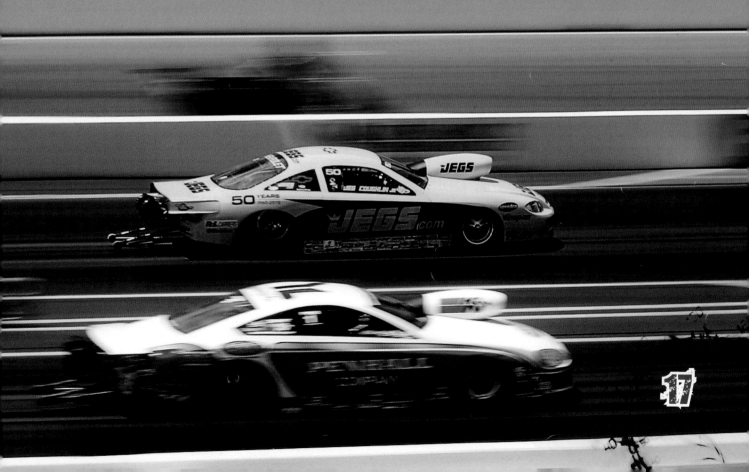

BETWEEN RACES

Another sort of race begins after the drag race is over. The car must be rebuilt! This takes up to 1¼ hours. Each team has up to six **mechanics**. Each mechanic has a job to do. The engine must be taken apart and have new parts put into it. The parachutes must be repacked and the car refueled. Any mistake in putting things back together could cause an accident in the next race. Computers are used to make sure everything works properly.

Jeg Coughlin's entire team of mechanics watches as he gets set for a race.

Fast Fact A racing series is a set of races for a certain type of vehicle. Pro Stock is one series in the National Hot Rod Association's (NHRA) Full Throttle Drag Racing Series.

19

In addition to the roll cage, each car has a driver-controlled system to stop fires. Safety workers can reach an accident in seconds to put out fires and get drivers out of their cars. Most tracks have doctors and ways to get hurt drivers to hospitals quickly. The Safety Safari is a crew of specially trained track workers who respond to accidents. Viewer safety is important, too. Modern racetracks are built to keep viewers out of the way of accidents on the track.

PRO STOCK NUMBERS

Quickest Win	6.509 seconds, Mike Edwards, 10/11/09
Fastest Speed	212 mph (341 kph), Greg Anderson, 03/29/10
Most Wins	97, Warren Johnson
First Pro Stock Champion	1974 (NHRA), Bob Glidden
Most NHRA Championships	10, Bob Glidden

GLOSSARY

fuel: something that is burned to create power

horsepower (HP): the measure of the power produced by an engine

hot rod: a street car that has been made to go faster and look cooler

IHRA: International Hot Rod Association, a major drag racing organization in the United States

mechanic: a person who works on cars

octane: the measure of stored energy in fuel

parachute: a specially shaped piece of cloth that collects air to slow something down

rev: to increase the speed of the engine

roll cage: a framework of metal bars around the driver

traction: the stickiness between two surfaces, such as a tire and the track

vehicle: an object that moves people from one place to another

V-8: an engine with two banks of four cylinders arranged in a V shape

weld: to join metal parts together by heating

FOR MORE INFORMATION

Books

NHRA Publications Staff. *The History of NHRA Pro Stock*. Glendora, CA: NHRA Publications, 2009.

Zuehlke, Jeffrey. *Drag Racers*. Minneapolis, MN: Lerner Publishing Group, 2008.

Web Sites

International Hot Rod Association (IHRA)
www.ihra.com
Read about drag racing at the Web site for the second-largest drag racing governing body.

The National Hot Rod Association (NHRA)
www.nhra.com
The Web site for the largest drag racing governing body has information on the hottest Pro Stock drivers.

INDEX